T0353759

Eating Clean
in *Costa Rica*

Chef Marie

Simple, Easy Recipes from the Kitchen of Blue Osa and Chef Marie

Balboa Press books may be ordered through booksellers or by contacting:

Balboa Press
A Division of Hay House
1663 Liberty Drive
Bloomington, IN 47403
www.balboapress.com
1 (877) 407-4847

Because of the dynamic nature of the Internet, any web addresses or links contained in this book may have changed since publication and may no longer be valid. The views expressed in this work are solely those of the author and do not necessarily reflect the views of the publisher, and the publisher hereby disclaims any responsibility for them.

Any people depicted in stock imagery provided by Thinkstock are models, and such images are being used for illustrative purposes only. Certain stock imagery © Thinkstock.

Artwork by Maria Hillier.

ISBN: 978-1-5043-3596-6 (sc)
ISBN: 978-1-5043-3597-3 (e)

Library of Congress Control Number: 2015910213

Print information available on the last page.

Balboa Press rev. date: 8/7/2015

BALBOA
PRESS
A DIVISION OF HAY HOUSE

Eating
Clean
in *Costa Rica*

They say, "There's nothing like Mom's cooking."

We say, "There's nothing like Marie's cooking!"

One of the original owners of the property, along with her late husband Jean- François. Marie was so inspired by Aaron and Adam's vision for Blue Osa that she remains the 'Mother' of the Blue Osa family several years later.

In my recipes, I use a pinch of originality, a spoonful of savoir faire and much, much love.

The jungle is where I cook. Here, I don't have the same ingredients that are available in big markets and city superstores.

So I use local products and created an original cuisine that combines influences from around the world with French flavours.

My cooking is simple, uncomplicated, flavourful and at times innovative.

I think that knowing how to eat is the beginning of knowing how to live. To know how to cook is to love to cook. So I encourage you to get playful at home in your own kitchen.

This cooking guide is dedicated to Adam, Aaron, my daughters, Katherine, Randy and Harriet… and to all of you who come to Blue Osa.

Love you!

Marie x

P.S. You will notice that many of my recipe ingredients are listed using grams and litres, which is the European way. The oven temperatures are also noted in Celcius rather than in Fahrenheit. I learned to cook measuring like this, but you may have not. Therefore, I have put a handy conversion table in the back of this book for you to use if you prefer to work with cups and ounces.

To find out more, visit: www.blueosa.com

Breakfast
and Brunch

A collection of brunch recipes to help you recall those precious mornings at Blue Osa & recreate them for yourself at home. Bon appétit.

Marie x

Zucchini Flan

Serves 8

Ingredients

½ teaspoon of baking powder
450 grams of zucchini, sliced into half moons
5 eggs
50 grams of crème fraiche (or sour cream)
3 tablespoons of flour (you can use gluten free with 1 teaspoon of corn starch)
½ teaspoon of curry powder
200 grams of feta cheese, cut into cubes
20 grams of grated parmesan cheese
3 cloves garlic, chopped
1 tablespoon of olive oil

Preparation

· Pre-heat the oven to 180 °C.
· Boil the zucchini in hot water for 5 minutes Drain and place in a bowl with salt and pepper, then add flour, curry powder, feta cheese, baking powder and garlic.
· In a separate bowl, beat the eggs, add crème fraiche or sour cream and olive oil. Slowly pour the liquid mixture into the bowl with the solid ingredients and mix well.

· Grease a shallow baking dish and pour in the flan mixture. Scatter the grated cheese on top.
· Place in the oven and bake for 35 minutes or until firm. Once cooked, allow to cool. Remove from the mold. Serve with spicy tomato sauce.

Breakfast & Brunch

Tuna and Pepper Cupcakes

Serves 4-6

Preparation

· Pre-heat oven to 375 °F.
· Sauté the peppers with the tuna in a pan.
· Drizzle with a little of the olive oil and add salt and pepper to taste. Cook lightly and remove from the heat. In a separate bowl, whisk together the eggs, flour, yeast, grated cheese, milk & remaining olive oil.
· Add the tuna and pepper mix. Stir.
· Once fully combined, fill muffin/cupcake tins.

· Bake in preheated oven for 20 minutes or until spongy.
· While cupcakes are baking, make the frosting by combining the cream cheese and sour cream in a small bowl.
· Put frosting into a pastry bag and decorate the cupcakes once cooled.

Ingredients

200 grams of canned tuna packed in water
500 grams of green peppers, chopped small
3 eggs
165 grams of flour
100 ml olive oil
25 ml milk
1 tablespoon of yeast
A small block of white cheese, grated
Salt and pepper

For the topping:
150 grams of cream cheese
2 large tablespoons of sour cream

Quiche Lorraine

Serves 6-8

Ingredients

1 pre-made pie crust
200 grams of smoked bacon, diced
150 grams of ham, diced
200 grams of grated cheese
100g Gruyère cheese
4 eggs
400 ml of sour cream
Pinch of paprika
Salt and pepper to taste

Preparation

· Pre-heat the oven to 180 °C.
· Place the dough in a pie plate.
· In a saucepan, blanch the bacon in boiling water for 1 minute then drain.
· Put the bacon in a frying pan without any fat and sauté 5 minutes on medium heat. Drain on paper towel, then dice.
· In a bowl, beat the eggs, cream, paprika, salt and pepper.
· Add the bacon, ham and cheese.
· Pour into the pie crust and sprinkle with gruyére.
· Place in oven and cook for 40 minutes.
· Allow quiche to cool for 10 minutes.

Spanish Tortilla Recipe

Serves 6-8

Preparation

- Pre-heat the oven to 180 °C.
- Wash and peel the potatoes, then slice into rounds.
- Heat the olive oil in a large pan on the stove and fry the potato rounds stirring constantly until they are tender and crisp.
- Beat the eggs together with salt and pepper.
- Add to the pan with the fried potatoes.
- Place in a hot oven and cook for 20 minutes until golden brown.
- Before serving, brush with a little olive oil and garnish with fresh herbs of your choice.

Ingredients

1 kg of potatoes
8 eggs
3 tablespoons of olive oil
Salt and pepper
Fresh herbs

Chocolate and Coconut Muffins

Makes 4

Ingredients

10 tablespoons flour
2 teaspoons of baking powder
8 tablespoons of sugar
6 tablespoons of coconut milk
4 tablespoons of oil
2 large eggs
6 tablespoons of shredded coconut, dried
12 squares of dark chocolate

Preparation

· Pre-heat the oven to 180 °C.
· Grease a tray of muffin molds.
· In a mixing bowl, beat the eggs with sugar until the mixture is well blended. Stir in the oil, then add flour & baking powder.
· Add the coconut milk & dried coconut.
· Pour part of the mixture into each of the muffin molds so that they are only half full.
· Take 1 piece of chocolate and place in the middle of the batter in each mold, then spoon over the remainder mixture to cover it.
· Place in the oven and bake for 15 minutes or until the muffins have risen and a toothpick comes away clean.
· Allow the muffins to cool, then place them on a tray for presentation and decorate with a little extra shredded coconut and/or cocoa powder.

Moist Banana Muffins

Serves 12

Preparation

- Pre-heat the oven to 180 °C.
- Grease the muffin molds.
- Crack the eggs into a mixing bowl and beat vigorously.
- Add the flour and butter.
  Add the baking powder, vanilla and salt and continue to beat the mixture until smooth.
- Peel and mash the bananas and add to the muffin mix.
- Stir thoroughly and spoon into the muffin molds.
- Place in the oven and bake for 25-30 minutes or until the muffins are golden and springy to the touch.
- Remove from the oven and allow to cool before serving.

Ingredients

3 to 4 ripe bananas
2 eggs
50 grams of butter, melted
150 grams of sugar
200 grams flour
1 pinch of salt
1 teaspoon of vanilla powder

Mango Muffins

Serves 12

Ingredients

300 grams of flour
2 ripe mangoes
100 grams of sugar
2 eggs
½ teaspoon baking powder
2 tablespoons of oil
21 ml of milk

Preparation

· Pre-heat the oven to 180 °C and grease the muffin molds.
· Peel and slice the mangoes and chop the flesh into small cubes.
· Mix all the ingredients in a large bowl, beating vigorously until the mixture is smooth.

· Pour batter into muffin molds and bake for 20 minutes or until the muffins are springy to the touch and lightly browned.
· Remove from the oven and allow to cool before placing on tray and serving.

Breakfast & Brunch

Main Dishes

Here are some of my absolute favourite fish and beef recipes, including two of my favorite tagines.

Marie x

Chicken Tagine with Prunes and Almonds

Serves 6

Ingredients

Clay tagine dish
1 large chicken, cut into pieces
2 or 3 onions
600 grams of prunes, pitted
80 grams of almonds
½ teaspoon of lemon juice
1 tablespoon of honey
½ teaspoon of cumin powder
½ teaspoon of cinnamon powder
½ teaspoon of ginger
2 teaspoons of sesame seeds
4 tablespoons of olive oil
Handful of chopped fresh cilantro
Salt and pepper

Preparation

· Pre-heat the oven to 190 °C.
· Peel and chop the onion.
· Cut the chicken into pieces.
· Heat the oil in a pan, then add the chicken and brown on all sides. Drain and remove.
· Add the onions in the same pan and cook with the juices for 5 minutes, stirring.
· Add the prunes, honey, lemon juice, all spices and the salt and pepper to the onion. Stir until smooth.
· Now add the chicken, plus ½ cup of hot water. Stir, then cover with the lid of the tagine.

· Bake in a hot oven for 40 minutes.
· During this time, dry roast the sesame seeds and almonds in a non- stick frying pan, stirring continuously until lightly browned. You don't need to use any oil.
· Just before the end of the cooking time, add the sesame seeds and almonds to the chicken dish.
· To serve, remove from the oven and decorate with a sprinkle of fresh cilantro.
· Serve with cumin couscous.

Main Dishes

Mango Chicken Tagine

Serves 4

Preparation

- Pre-heat your oven to 200 °C.
- Peel and chop the onions, cook lightly in a pan using a little oil. Reserve and keep to one side.
- Peel the mangoes, cut into two, remove the stones and cut into thin slices. Cook the mangoes lightly in a little oil, reserve and keep to one side for later.
- Slice chicken thighs into chunky strips and fry the chicken pieces to dry for a few minutes in a pan.
- Coat the tagine with oil first, add the spices (paprika ginger. saffron, cinnamon) and mix well.

- Next place the cooked mango into the tangine with the lemon juice and then the cooked onion.
- Then place the chicken on top and finally pour a glass of water over it. Season with salt and pepper.
- Stir gently, then cover the tagine with the lid.
- Place in the oven for 30 minutes to cook through and serve contents over white rice.

Ingredients

A clay tagine dish
4 chicken thighs
3 onions, chopped
3 large mangoes (partially ripe)
1 lemon, juiced
3 tablespoons fresh cilantro, finely chopped
2 tablespoons of olive oil
½ teaspoon of paprika powder
½ teaspoon of ginger powder
1 teaspoon of saffron
A pinch of cinnamon powder
Salt and black pepper

Chicken Basquaise

Serves 4

Ingredients

1 chicken
1 kg of tomatoes
3 cloves of garlic, crushed
3 onions, diced
700 grams of red pepper
1 bouquet garni (thyme, rosemary, bay leaf)
3 tablespoons of olive oil
Salt and pepper
A pinch of chili powder

Preparation

· Cut the chicken into pieces. Cut the peppers, de-seed and slice.
· Crush the garlic and dice the onion.
· Peel the tomatoes. For easier peeling make an indentation in each tomato and scald in hot water for 1 to 2 minutes. The skin should then slide off easily.
· Chop the tomatoes and eliminate any hard parts.

· Warm the olive oil in a pan and on a low heat add the garlic,onion, red pepper and chicken. Cook for 5 minutes, stirring with a wooden spoon.
· Add the tomatoes, seasoning and spice and cook for another 20 minutes.

Main Dishes

Coconut Chicken

Preparation

- Wash the lime in hot water and then grate its zest.
- Fry the chicken in a wok pan with lime zest, onions and a little oil.
- Add the garlic and tomato paste.
- Pour in the coconut milk.
- Reduce the heat and let simmer 20 minutes.
- When the chicken is cooked, add the lime juice and season to taste.
- Serve with basmati rice and fresh pineapple.

Ingredients

800 grams of chicken
200 grams of fresh pineapple
200 ml of coconut milk
1-2 onions
2 cloves garlic, chopped
2 limes, juiced and zested
½ teaspoon of ground cinnamon
1 tablespoon of concentrated tomato paste
1 tablespoon of olive oil

Chicken Yassa

Serves 6

Ingredients

1 large chicken
8-10 onions, chopped
4 lemons, juiced
3 tablespoons of peanut oil
2 teaspoons of dijon mustard (fresh)
2 cubes of chicken bouillon
1 or 2 dried chilies, chopped
Salt & pepper to taste

Preparation

· Prepare a marinade by mixing the mustard, oil, lemon juice, salt and pepper.
· Cut the chicken into pieces, then brush it with the marinade.
· In a large mixing bowl, combine the remaining marinade with the onions. Marinade the chicken and onions in the fridge (separately) for 3 hours.

· Heat the oil in a wok and brown the chicken pieces on high heat. Add onions and sauté on low heat for 10 minutes. As soon as the onions have browned, add the cubes of bouillon, 2 glasses of water and the chilies. Mix and leave to cook for 40-45 minutes over medium heat. Season to taste and serve.

Main Dishes

Roast Chicken

Serves 4

Preparation

- Pre-heat the oven to 220 °C.
- Make a mixture with the garlic, butter, half the thyme and a little oil.
- Massage the chicken thoroughly with the mixture.
- Place in a big roasting pan and drizzle with lemon juice.
- Peel the potatoes and cut into thick wedges and arrange them around the chicken. Cover in olive oil, salt, pepper and the leftover thyme.
- Roast in the oven for 1 hour and 15 minutes until the chicken is crisp and brown and the potatoes are roasted.

Serve with tomato and avocado salad.

Ingredients

One large chicken
600 grams of potatoes
1 head of garlic, all cloves crushed
A bunch of fresh thyme, chopped, or 1 tablespoon of dried thyme
1 teaspoon of lemon juice
3 tablespoons of olive oil
1 tablespoon of melted butter
1 glass of water
Salt and pepper

Fish with Avocado Sauce

Serves 4

Ingredients

4 Mahi Mahi fillets (or other firm white fish)
2 tablespoons of olive oil
Salt and pepper

For the sauce:
1 avocado
1 tablespoon of lemon juice
100 ml of sour cream
10 grams butter
1 clove garlic
Salt and pepper

Preparation

· Rinse and pat dry the fish. Pour the olive oil in a dish and add the fish. Add pepper and leave the fillets to marinate for 25 minutes.

For the sauce:
· Peel and pit the avocado. Mash the flesh until smooth.
· Peel and crush the garlic.
· Melt the butter in a heavy saucepan and fry the garlic for about 1 minute on low heat.
· Add the avocado flesh and lemon juice.

· Simmer for a few minutes on low heat, without boiling, stirring occasionally.
· Remove from heat and keep warm.
· Place the fillets on the grill and cook on each side for 2-3 minutes.
· Once cooked, put on a plate and drizzle with a generous coating of the avocado sauce.

Main Dishes

Fish a' la Provençale

Serves 6

Preparation

- Finely chop the onion and crush the garlic.
- Pour the olive oil in a pan and sauté both together.
- Cut the tomatoes and peppers into strips and add them to the pan.
- Add the bouquet garni and black olives.
- Mix everything together thoroughly and stir in the white wine.
- Dip fish pieces into the sauce and cook on a low heat for 10 minutes.
- Serve with boiled potatoes and slices of baguette grilled with garlic.

Ingredients

1 kg of Mahi Mahi or Corbina
500 grams of ripe tomatoes
4 peppers (2 red and 2 green)
3 onions, chopped
2 cloves garlic
4 tablespoons of olive oil
A bouquet garni
(thyme, rosemary and bay leaf)
1 cup of black olives
A glass of dry white wine
Salt and black pepper to taste

Mahi Mahi Balinese Style

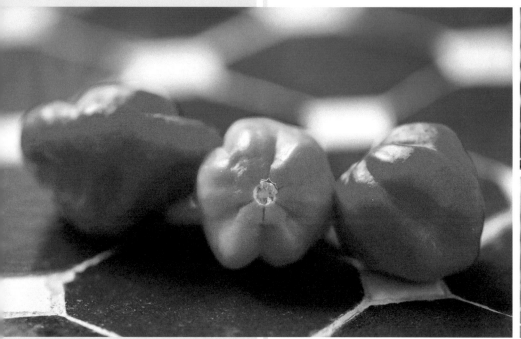

Serves 6

Ingredients

1 kg of fish fillets, ideally Mahi Mahi
1 glass of coconut milk
1 small red pepper, julienned
2 onions, chopped finely
4 cloves garlic, minced
30 grams of fresh ginger, crushed
2 teaspoons of red curry paste
3 tablespoons of sesame oil
For the accompaniment
1 avocado
1 mango
1 cup of coconut chips
150 grams of cashew nuts
A few raisins

Preparation

· Prepare the ingredients.
· Wash the fish and cut into chunks.
· Sweat the onion, garlic and ginger with a little oil in a wok.
· Add the red curry paste and coconut milk, then simmer for a few minutes.
· Add the fish and red pepper, and stir.
· Add salt and pepper to taste.
· Cook, covered, 15 minutes.
· Serve the fish curry in a large dish accompanied by white rice.

· In small porcelain bowls, present the coconut chips, avocado, diced mango, raisins and roasted cashew nuts as a garnish to add a mouthwatering combination of texture and flavor to the fish.

Main Dishes

Caribbean Style Fish with Orange Ginger Salad

Serves 4

Preparation

The Fish

- Fry the fillets in a pan on a medium heat with a pat of butter.
- Add the sliced peppers, garlic, chopped parsley, paprika, salt and pepper.
- Simmer gently for 5-6 minutes, turning the fish to ensure it is done on both sides.
- Add the mango and brown sugar.
- Brown some sliced mango.
- At the last moment, add a pinch of brown sugar so it all starts to caramelize.
- Serve immediately.

Orange Ginger salad

- Remove the orange rind and cut into segments.
- Peel the ginger and cut it into thin strips.
- Add the ginger to the orange.
- Add the Stevia powder and cinnamon, then mix together well and refrigerate until serving.

Ingredients

The Fish:
4 fillets of Mahi Mahi or Corbina
A large pat of butter
A few slices of red, yellow and green peppers
1-2 cloves of garlic, crushed
A little fresh parsley
A pinch of paprika
1 ripe mango, sliced
A pinch of brown sugar
Salt and pepper

Orange Ginger salad:
2 oranges
10 grams of fresh ginger
½ teaspoon chopped mint
A pinch of cinnamon
½ teaspoon Stevia powder

Coconut Encrusted Mahi Mahi

Serves 6

Ingredients

6 fillets of Mahi Mahi
2 cups of flour
3 eggs, beaten
3 cups of shredded dried coconut
3 cups of coconut milk if you have it
(if not, regular milk can be used)
1 tablespoon of salt
1 tablespoon of pepper
Oil for frying

Preparation

· Refrigerate the Mahi Mahi for 3 hours prior to cooking.
· Beat the eggs together with the milk, salt and pepper in a bowl. Place flour on one plate.
· Place the coconut on a separate plate.
· Take one piece of fish at a time and dip it first in the egg mixture, then dip in the flour and then the coconut (coating both sides evenly).
· In a large frying pan, add some oil and keep the heat medium to high. Fry the fish on both sides for around 5 minutes each until browned.
· Once cooked transfer to a plate covered with a kitchen towel to absorb the oil before serving.
· Serve with fresh mango salsa & tabasco sauce.

Main Dishes

Puttanesca Sauce for Pasta

Serves 4

Preparation

- Heat the oil in large skillet or saucepan.
- Add the garlic, chili and anchovies.
- Cook for 1 minute.
- Add tomatoes, olives and capers.
- Bring to a boil, then reduce heat and let simmer about 20 minutes to get a smooth sauce.
- Pour over hot pasta.

Ingredients

3 tablespoons of olive oil

2 cloves of crushed garlic

1 dried red chili, crushed

6 anchovy fillets

500 grams tomatoes, peeled, seeded and chopped

125 grams of black olives, halved

2 tablespoons of capers

Beef Bourguignon

Serves 4

Ingredients

2 kilograms of beef, cut into chunks
250 grams of bacon, cubed
1½ glasses of red wine
1-2 onions
400 grams of mushrooms, sliced
150 grams of butter
1 sprig of thyme
A handful of basil
A handful of parsley
2 or 3 bay leaves
A little nutmeg
2 tablespoons of oil
2 tablespoons of flour
2 cloves garlic, cut into chunky slices
2 teaspoons of Dijon mustard
3 or 4 carrots, cut into batons
Salt and pepper

Preparation

· First we prepare the marinade – do this phase the day before eating.
· Peel the onion and finely chop.
· Make a bouquet garni with the herbs, chopping them finely (you may also like to add a little fresh basil if you have it).
· Cut the meat into large cubes. Place in large bowl, drizzle the olive oil and red wine over the meat. Add the herbs, onion, carrots, salt, pepper, a little nutmeg and garlic before covering in plastic wrap.
· Refrigerate for 18 hours.
· The next day, remove meat from marinade and drain well with a strainer - keep the strained marinade in a separate bowl.
· Melt 75 grams of butter and a little oil in a skillet over high heat. When it's melted, add the meat, plus the bacon and cook for 2-3 minutes to seal the juices. Once it begins to brown, add the flour. Add the marinade and stir.
· Bring to a boil, add another pinch of flour, reduce to low heat then simmer.
· Cook for 2 hours, stirring occasionally.
· Add the mustard and mushrooms and some fresh basil 20 minutes before the end of the cooking time.
· To serve, garnish with some freshly chopped parsley. Serve with mashed potatoes or pasta.

Costa Rica Dishes

I just couldn't write my cookbook without talking about some Costa Rican recipes, very simple and tasty, really close to nature - with vegetables, fruits, and fish -- that we foreigners know embody the Tico way of life: Pura Vida.

Marie x

Costa Rican Gallo Pinto

Serves 4

Ingredients

2 tablespoons oil
½ onion, finely chopped
½ red bell pepper, finely chopped
1 15 oz can (or 425 grams)
of cooked black beans, drained
3 cups "day old" cooked rice*
(200 grams un-cooked)
1½ tablespoons Worcestershire Sauce
4 tablespoons broth
(ideally beef, but chicken will do)
½ tablespoon Tabasco Sauce, optional
1 handful of cilantro, finely chopped
6 strips bacon, cooked, drained, crumbled.
Reserve a little for garnish.
Salt and pepper

Preparation

· In a pan, sauté the onion and bell pepper in oil on medium heat. Add beans and cook for 2 minutes.
· Add cooked rice and mix, cook for 3 minutes or more.
· Add the Worcestershire Sauce, Tabasco Sauce, broth, cilantro, and bacon. Mix well. Season with salt and pepper. If the rice seems too dry, add a bit more broth.
· Garnish with reserved bacon crumbs.
· If desired, top with sour cream.

* 200 grams (1 cup) of uncooked rice yields about 3 cups cooked. Best with Jasmine rice, but other white rices such as basmati also work well. If you're making your rice the same day, pop it into the refrigerator for a bit to give it a chance to "age."

Costa Rican Dishes

Black Bean Soup

Serves 6

Preparation

- Soak black beans overnight.
- Cook black beans in pan of salt water for 45 minutes.
- Drain the beans
- In a pot, add 6 cups of water, salt, cilantro, onion and garlic. Simmer for 30 minutes.
- Add Worcestershire sauce to the pot and simmer on low heat.
- Purée the mixture.
- Serve in bowls and garnish with tortilla chips.

Ingredients

2 cups dried black beans

6 cups of water

1 onion, finely chopped

2 cloves garlic, finely chopped

1 teaspoon salt

2 tablespoon of fresh cilantro, finely chopped

1 tablespoon of Worcestershire Sauce

Chicken and Rice

Serves 8

Ingredients

1 chicken, cut up
400 grams rice
1-2 onions, finely chopped
1 green bell pepper, finely chopped
½ cup cooked peas
½ cup cooked carrots, diced
½ cup cooked green beans, sliced
2 tablespoons raisins
2 tablespoons green olives, sliced
2 teaspoons of Worcestershire sauce
2 tablespoons of oil
Salt to taste
Fresh cilantro

Preparation

· Cook the chicken in a pan with ½ the onion and ½ the bell pepper, salt, and 4 cups of water until tender. Let cool.
· Strain the remaining liquid and add water to make 5 cups.
· Discard the bones and shred the chicken.
· In a large pot, heat the oil and sauté the remaining onion and pepper.

· Add the rice, vegetables, chicken stock, shredded chicken, and water mixture.
· Bring to a boil then simmer til rice is done. Add raisins and olives.
· Fluff with a fork.

Costa Rican Dishes

Cabbage Salad

Serves 6

Preparation

· Mix all ingredients together in a large bowl.
· Serve immediately in 6 small bowls.

Ingredients

2 cups cabbage, shredded
1 cup ripe tomato, diced
3 tablespoons of fresh cilantro, finely chopped
2 teaspoons lemon juice
2 teaspoons of olive oil
A pinch of salt
Fresh cracked black pepper to taste

Plantain Picadillo

Serves 8

Ingredients

4 green plantains cut into threes
¼ kg ground beef
2 tablespoons onions, finely chopped
2 tablespoons fresh cilantro, finely chopped
2 cloves garlic, finely chopped
½ cup tomato, minced
1 teaspoon of Worcestershire sauce
1½ teaspoons of salt
½ teaspoon of fresh cracked pepper
Dash of Tabasco
Oil

Preparation

· Peel plantains and cut into three pieces each.
· Cook in pot of water with 1 teaspoon of salt until tender.
· Let cool, mince and set aside.
· In a large skillet, cook the meat with onion, garlic, salt and pepper, using the oil as needed.
· When done, add remaining ingredients and cook for 10 minutes before serving.

Costa Rican Dishes

Patacones

Serves 6-8

Preparation

- Peel the plantains and cut in 1/2 inch rounds.
- Fry in hot oil until golden.
- Scoop out of hot oil with slotted spoon.
- Place on cutting board and smash the plantains with a flat surface or rolling pin.
- Sprinkle with salt and return to pan to fry again, until crispy.
- Drain on paper towels and serve immediately.
- Can be served with guacamole or black bean dip.

Ingredients

4 green plantains cut into rounds
Pinch of salt
Oil

Frijoles Molido (Black Bean Dip)

Serves 4-6

Ingredients

500 grams cooked black beans
(canned beans are okay)
1 teaspoon vegetable oil
1 small onion, finely chopped
2 cloves garlic, minced
A handful of cilantro leaves, finely chopped
½-1 teaspoon of Tabasco or other hot sauce
1 tablespoon of sugar
1 ½ tablespoon of Worcestershire sauce
1 tablespoon of salt
Fresh lime juice to taste
Large bag of tortilla chips

Preparation

· In a blender, food processor or with a potato masher, blend the beans until creamy but leave some texture.
· Place mashed beans in a large mixing bowl.
· In a small frying pan, heat the oil and sauté the onion for 2 minutes.
· Add the garlic and cook for 30 seconds.

· Add the black beans along with cilantro, hot sauce, sugar, Worcestershire sauce and salt.
· Mix well and season to taste with salt and lime juice.
· Serve with tortilla chips.

Costa Rican Dishes

Chayote Picadillo

Serves 8

Preparation

- On medium / high heat, sauté the ground meat in oil with onion, garlic, salt and pepper until lightly brown.
- Add remaining ingredients, cover and cook until chayote is tender.
- Serve hot.

Ingredients

3 chayotes, peeled and diced
450 grams of ground beef
1 onion, finely chopped
2 tablespoons of cilantro, finely chopped
2 cloves garlic, finely chopped
Fresh cracked pepper
1 tablespoon of oil

Stuffed Chayote

Serves 4

Ingredients

2 small chayote, halved
1 can of tuna in oil, drained
2 tablespoons of grated Gruyère cheese
A little stale bread
1 lime, juiced
Milk
Olive oil
Salt and pepper to season

Preparation

- Pre-heat the oven to 350 °F.
- Halve the chayote lengthwise. Place the pieces in a pot of water and bring to boil.
- Cover and simmer for 10-15 minutes until tender, then drain.
- Allow to cool, then remove the seeds. Scoop out the flesh / pulp leaving ¼ inch chayote.
- Turn chayote upside down and set aside to drain.
- Chop the scooped out flesh/pulp and put in a mixing bowl. Add the tuna, lime juice and season.
- In another bowl, soak the stale bread in milk until soft and then combine it with the rest of the ingredients. Mix well.
- Scoop the mixture into the chayote shells, drizzle with olive oil and sprinkle with cheese. Place in the oven to bake until the cheese is melted and lightly brown.
- Serve on plates with Creole rice.

Coconut Flan

Serves 10-12

Preparation

· Pre-heat the oven to 180 °C.
· Mix the eggs and sugar in a blender until smooth.
· Add the milk and coconut and blend well. Pour into a glass baking dish.
· Put this into a larger baking dish and add water until half way up sides of smaller baking dish. Bake for 45 minutes.

· To test, stick a toothpick into the flan. If it comes out clean, the flan is ready. Remove from oven.
· Allow the flan to cool. Refrigerate before serving. Ideally the flan is served chilled.

Ingredients

1 litre milk
100 grams of sugar
75 grams fresh coconut
8 eggs

Vegetarian Dishes

I looked for recipes that inspire you to cook delicious meals with ingredients that are healthy, balanced, economical and sustainable. Indian traditional cooking is rich with vegetarian dishes so it seems natural for a yoga retreat to make vegetarian recipes with love.

Marie x

Indonesian Coconut Rice

Serves 4

Preparation

- Thinly slice the scallion/spring onion.
- Heat the oil in a wok, add the peanuts and stir frequently until golden brown.
- Add shredded coconut and stir until lightly browned and fragrant.
- Pour the coconut milk and 500 ml of water into the wok.
- Add the rice, lemongrass, curry powder and scallion/spring onion and bring to a boil. Simmer for 2 minutes. Add the cumin, cardamom and turmeric and bring to a boil again. Remove the lemongrass.
- Cover, lower the heat and continue cooking for 10 minutes or until rice is tender and all the liquid has been absorbed.
- Serve warm.

Ingredients

2 scallions / spring onions sliced thinly
1 tablespoon of vegetable oil
80 grams of chopped peanuts
1 tablespoon of shredded coconut
250 ml of coconut milk
10 cm lemongrass
1 teaspoon of curry powder
1 teaspoon of cumin
½ teaspoon of cardamom
½ teaspoon of turmeric
500 grams of long grain rice

Tofu with Peas

Serves 4

Ingredients

600 grams of tofu, cubed
400 grams Asian mushrooms
(shiitake, oyster, etc.)
4 tablespoons of peanut oil
2 teaspoons of chili paste
2 cloves garlic, finely chopped
300 grams of pea pods
4 tablespoons of soy sauce
Salt and pepper to season

Preparation

· Trim the pea pods. Cut the tofu into 2 cm cubes and cut the mushrooms into slices.
· Heat 2 tablespoons of oil in a wok over high heat, sauté the tofu in two batches for 2 or 3 minutes just until they are evenly browned. Transfer browned tofu onto a plate.
· Heat the rest of the oil in the pan. Add the chili paste, garlic, pea pods, mushrooms and a tablespoon of water.

· Sauté everything together for a few minutes, stirring until the vegetables are almost cooked but still crisp.
· Put the tofu in the wok, pour in the soy sauce and sauté for one minute further.
· Serve immediately in a bowl with cooked rice.

Vegetarian Phad Thai

Serves 4

Preparation

- Soak rice noodles in hot water for 15 minutes. Drain and set aside.
- Cut the pepper into strips and cut the onion diagonally into small slices.
- Chop the tofu into strips 5 mm wide and slice the scallions thinly.
- Prepare the sauce. Mix the soy sauce, the lime juice, the sugar and the chili paste.
- In a wok on high heat, heat the oil and cook the eggs for 30 seconds like an omelette. Remove and cut into strips. In the heated wok, heat the rest of the oil and add the onions, garlic and pepper and cook for 2-3 minutes or until the onions are tender.
- Add the noodles and stir.
- Blend the eggs, scallions, tofu and half of the cilantro.
- Add the sauce and mix to cover the noodles. Top with bean sprouts, peanuts, and the rest of the cilantro. Serve immediately.

Ingredients

400 grams of rice noodles
1 small red pepper
6 scallions/spring onions
100 grams of firm tofu, cut into cubes
1 onion, chopped fine
2 tablespoons of peanut oil
2 eggs, slightly beaten
2 cloves garlic, crushed
25 grams of fresh cilantro, chopped
90 grams bean sprouts
40 grams of peanuts, chopped and roasted

For the sauce
4 tablespoons of soy sauce
2 tablespoons of lime juice
1 tablespoon of brown sugar
2 teaspoons of chili paste

Chocolate Laced Mexican Beans

Serves 4-6

Ingredients

250 grams red beans, cooked
1 small onion, diced
2-3 garlic cloves, crushed
5 tablespoons of tomato concentrate
½ teaspoon of chili powder
1 pinch of cumin
1 pinch of cayenne pepper
1 tablespoon of high-cocoa content, cocoa powder
Salt and pepper to taste
1 teaspoon of brown sugar
Olive oil

Preparation

· In a frying pan sauté the onion and garlic in olive oil.
· Add the beans and stir in all the spices, including the cocoa, sugar and seasoning.
· Add the tomato concentrate.
· Add a little water if needed and simmer on a gentle heat for 25 minutes.
· Serve with fresh tortillas, a fresh tomato salad, guacamole and white rice on a plate.

Vegetarian Dishes

Baked Potato with Cottage Cheese and Herbs

Serves 4

Preparation

· Pre-heat the oven to 375 °F.
· Wash and dry the potatoes, pierce the flesh and dust with a little salt and pepper and wrap in foil.
· Bake in the oven for 1 hour.
· In the meantime, combine the cottage cheese, milk, herbs and spices in a bowl. Mix until smooth.

· Remove the potatoes from the oven, un-wrap and serve piping hot on a plate with a generous dollop of the herbal cream cheese.
· Serve with a large green salad.

Ingredients

4 large potatoes
500 grams of cottage cheese, fat free
2 onions, chopped finely
1 large cucumber
1 generous bunch of chives
1 teaspoon of green peppercorns, crushed
1-2 tablespoons of milk
Salt and pepper to season

Tofu Yassa

Serves 2

Ingredients

100 grams of firm tofu
1 lime, juiced
1 onion, chopped
2 teaspoons of mustard powder
2 tablespoons of olive oil
1 tomato, chopped
1 pepper, chopped
A handful of coriander
Salt and pepper to season

Preparation

· Cut the tofu into cubes.
· Make a marinade with the lime, mustard and olive oil.
· Brush the tofu with half of the marinade (save other half for later use) and refrigerate for an hour.
· Sauté the onion, tomato, pepper and coriander. When the onion becomes soft, add the remaining marinade.
· Add the tofu, stir well and simmer for 10-15 minutes.
· Serve with steamed quinoa.

Vegetarian Dishes

Indian Style Tofu

Serves 4

Preparation

· Heat the oil in a pan, add the cumin, bay leaf, pepper corns and cloves.
· Add the onion and simmer for 10 minutes or until they are soft and muddled with the spices.
· Add the tofu, cover and cook for an additional 10 minutes.
· Add the garlic, ginger and remaining spices.
· Add the tomato and a little water if needed.
· Simmer for 10 minutes and serve with a little sprinkle of
chopped cilantro.

Ingredients

100 grams of cubed firm tofu
1 tomato, diced
250 grams of onions, sliced thinly
1-2 teaspoons of cumin
1 teaspoon of turmeric
1 teaspoon of curry powder
1 teaspoon of paprika
1 clove of garlic, crushed
2 cm piece of ginger, grated
A handful of fresh cilantro
1 bay leaf
2 cloves
Oil
Salt to season
A little water

Tapas

In Biarritz, I live near Spain where they make Tapas to share with friends. Slices of bread, nan, tacos, pita bread, rice crackers with guacamole, eggplant caviar, hummus, tapenade, etc. You can make delicious Tapas that all your friends will love.

Marie x

Green Olive Tapenade

Serves 10

Preparation

· Place the olives, anchovies, almonds and
  capers in a blender or food processor.
· Start blending and slowly add the olive oil,
  a little at a time.
· Add the lemon juice if desired.
· Pour into a beautiful bowl and serve with
  blinis or toasted French baguette.

Ingredients

200 grams of green olives, pitted
(you can use black olives as an alternative)
10 anchovy filets
50 grams of blanched almonds
50 grams capers
2 tablespoons olive oil
Juice of 1 lemon (optional)
Salt and pepper to season

Blinis

Serves 10

Ingredients

1 kg flour
25 grams yeast
230 ml of milk
5 eggs
100 grams salted butter or vegetable oil

Preparation

- Warm the milk gently and pour into a mixing bowl.
- Add the yeast and flour, then stir.
- Let the mix sit for 1 hour and 15 minutes.
- In two bowls, separate the eggs, setting the whites aside.
- Take the yolks and mix into the batter.
- Mix well and cover with a dish cloth and let it sit for another hour.
- Melt butter or oil in pan then slowly stir into batter.
- Whisk the egg whites into stiff peaks and gently fold them into the batter.
- Lightly oil a pan using a paper towel and place on a high heat.
- When the pan is hot, add small ladles of batter and cook. Flip onto the other side once you see tiny bubbles start to form.
- Serve on a plate with olive tapenade, pâté, caviar, smoked salmon, etc.

Tapas

Pesto Muffins

 ## Preparation

- Pre-heat the oven to 200 °C.
- Grease a muffin tray.
- In a large bowl, mix the flour, baking soda and salt.
- In another bowl, mix the egg, olive oil and the milk.
- Pour wet mixture into bowl with flour and stir.
- Add the pesto and stir again.
- Once batter is thoroughly mixed, fill each mold ¾ full and sprinkle with pine nuts.
- Place the muffin tray in the oven and bake for 25 minutes or until lightly browned.
- Remove from the oven and allow to cool before turning out, and serve.

Ingredients

125 grams flour
100 grams toasted pine nuts
1 teaspoon baking powder
Pinch of salt
1 egg
2 tablespoons of olive oil
120 ml of milk
3 tablespoons of pesto

Tomato Bruschetta

Serves 5

Ingredients

Fresh tomato sauce
1 fresh French baguette
150 grams of Gruyère cheese, grated
Handful of black olives

Preparation

· Pre-heat the oven to 375 °F.
· Cut the baguette into 2cm slices diagonally and place on a baking tray.
· Spoon a little tomato sauce over each bread slice.
· Sprinkle with some cheese and top with a sliced black olive.
· Place in the oven for 5-10 minutes until the bread is crusty around the edges and the cheese has melted.
· Serve warm or cold. Both are equally divine!

Tapas

Eggplant Caviar

Serves 8

Preparation

- Pre-heat the oven to 330 °F.
- Cut the ends off and slice the eggplant lengthways in half.
- Sprinkle with salt, pepper and garlic.
- Put the halves back together and wrap in aluminum foil.
- Drizzle with olive oil before sealing the ends.
- Place on a baking tray and bake for 1 hour.
- Remove from the oven and let rest for 5 minutes before unwrapping.

- Scoop the flesh from the eggplant and into a food processor.
- Add the lemon juice and 1 teaspoon of olive oil.
- Season to taste with salt and pepper.
- Purée the mix together until smooth.
- Serve cold on sliced baguette or blinis.
- Garnish with Feta crumbles (optional).

Ingredients

2 large eggplants
4 tablespoons olive oil
3 garlic cloves, crushed
Juice of half a lemon
Salt and pepper
Feta crumbles (optional)

Ceviche Mahi Mahi

Serves 4

Ingredients

500 grams of fresh Mahi Mahi
5 fresh tomatoes, chopped
4 lemons, juiced
Half large onion, chopped
¼ cup of fresh cilantro
3 tablespoons of olive oil
10 black olives, pitted and chopped
1 avocado, chopped small
Pinch of salt
Pinch dried oregano
Tabasco to taste

Preparation

- Cut the Mahi Mahi into small slices or strips and place in a bowl.
- Add the juice of 2 lemons.
- Marinate for one hour.
- Remove the fish from the lemon juice and place in a separate bowl.
- Add the onions to the fish and mix.
- Add the juice of the remaining two lemons and the remaining ingredients.
- Mix well and serve in a bowl or dish.
- Soda crackers and sliced baguette make the perfect accompaniment.

Tapas

Green Pea Hummus

Serves 6

 ## Preparation

- Boil a big pot of lightly salted water. Add the peas and cook just until tender. Remove and let cool.
- Put the garlic through a garlic press. Zest and juice the lemons. Set these to one side.
- In a food processor, add the almonds and pulse to chop coarsely. Reserve them in a small bowl.
- In a food processor, put the peas, garlic, lemon juice and lemon zest, plus salt and pepper to taste.

- Mix well and slowly pour the olive oil into the food processor until fully blended. Add more olive oil if too thick. Pour into a bowl and stir in the mint and the almonds by hand. Cover and refrigerate.
- Serve with slices of toasted baguette.

Ingredients

300 grams peas (fresh, canned or frozen)
½ garlic clove
2 lemons
25 grams of almonds
3 tablespoons of olive oil
2 tablespoons of fresh mint, chopped
Salt and pepper to taste

Hummus

Serves 6

Ingredients

150 grams cooked chick peas,
jarred or canned

1 tablespoon of tahini (organic grocery
stores or Oriental).

If not available, grind 2 tablespoons of
sesame seeds in a coffee grinder.

3 tablespoons of olive oil

1 lemon, juiced

1 clove garlic, crushed

Salt and pepper

Preparation

· Rinse the chickpeas under running water.
  Let them drain.

· Brown the ground tahini (or sesame seeds)
  in a nonstick skillet with no fat, 2 to 3
  minutes.

· Place all the ingredients into a blender and
  blend together until smooth. If it gets too
  thick, add a bit more olive oil.

· Pour into a dish, drizzle with olive oil and/
  or black pepper or paprika.

Guacamole

Serves 6

Preparation

- Remove the pits and scoop the flesh of avocado and place in a blender or mixing bowl.
- Add the finely chopped onion, cayenne pepper and salt.
- Mix in blender or use hand blender or mash with a potato masher.
- Add the chopped tomatoes and herbs and mix together with a wooden spoon.
- Place in a dish to serve and garnish with a little extra chopped cilantro.

Ingredients

3 avocados, ripe
1 lime, juiced
1 tomato, chopped
1 onion, chopped finely
2 teaspoons of cayenne pepper
1 small handful fresh cilantro
Pinch of salt

Tzatziki

Serves 6

Ingredients

2 cucumbers
2 small 125 gram pots of Greek yoghurt or
thick natural yoghurt
Pinch of cumin powder
Salt and white pepper
Fresh mint leaves to garnish

Preparation

· Peel and grate the cucumbers.
· Place into a sieve and set over a bowl to let
  the cucumber water drain out.
· In a separate bowl, combine the remaining
  ingredients together and stir, seasoning to
  taste.
· Mix in the grated cucumber flesh, cover
  and cool in the fridge.
· Garnish with fresh mint leaves to serve.
· This is ideal on toasted baguette.

Onion Chutney

Serves 6

 ## Preparation

- Cut the onions in half and thinly slice.
- Heat the oil in the pan.
- Add the onions. Let them brown on a low heat.
- When they begin to brown, add the sugar, a little salt, stir and continue cooking until slightly caramelized.
- Add the ras el-hanout and cook a minute or two longer.
- Let cool, cover and refrigerate until ready to serve.
- Serve on toasted, sliced baguette. Perfect!

Ingredients

6 red onions
3 tablespoons of olive oil
1 tablespoon of sugar
1 tablespoon of ras el-hanout
(Moroccan spice blend)
Pinch of salt

Mango Ceviche

Serves 10

Ingredients

4-5 ripe mangoes
1 tablespoon of lemon juice
½ small onion, finely chopped
¼ of black pepper
½ salt
1 teaspoons of Worcestershire sauce

 ## Preparation

· Cut the mangoes in half and score out the flesh.
· Chop into small cubes and in a bowl combine with the rest of the ingredients.
· Refrigerate to cool.
· Serve with tortilla chips or crackers.

Mango Chutney

Serves 10

 Preparation

- Peel and coarsely chop the mangoes.
- In a bowl, add all ingredients to the mangoes except cilantro.
- Let marinade for one hour.
- Put ingredients in large pot and bring to a boil.
- Reduce heat and simmer uncovered for an hour.
- Add chopped cilantro in the last 10 minutes.
- Put into small jars, let cool, cover and place in refrigerator.
- Wait 2-3 days before eating.
- Good for up to 6 months.

Ingredients

600 grams of fresh mango
250 grams of brown sugar
1 teaspoon of turmeric
250 ml of red wine vinegar
250 grams of onion, coarsely chopped
½ lime, peeled and finely chopped
125 grams of freshly grated ginger
125 grams orange, peeled
and finely chopped
175 grams of raisins

125 grams honey
60 grams of lemon, peeled
and finely chopped
3 cloves of garlic, minced
1 tablespoons of whole mustard seed
1 teaspoon of cayenne
1 teaspoon of cinnamon
A pinch of red pepper flakes
2 tablespoons of fresh cilantro

Potato Croquette with Pesto and Green Papaya

Serves 6

Ingredients

1 egg
7 medium potatoes sliced
½ medium green papaya (or 1 carrot)
2 tablespoons of flour
100 grams of Gruyère cheese, grated
Salt and pepper
2 medium bunches of mesclun
(small mixed salad)
2 cloves garlic, crushed
1 tablespoon of almonds
2 tablespoons of olive oil
30 grams of Parmesan, grated
Vegetable oil for frying

Preparation

- Mix the salad in a bowl. Put Parmesan, chopped garlic and almonds in a food processor and mix until a paste is formed. Slowly drizzle in the olive oil.
- Place cut potatoes in a pot and boil until tender. Drain water and mash. Add the cheese and mix together well.
- Add the grated papaya or carrot. Mix again and add salt and pepper to taste.
- Form patties with the potato mash and dust with flour.
- Heat a frying pan on a high heat and add enough oil for frying. Add the patties in batches and fry until crisp and golden on both sides.
- Place croquettes on paper towels to absorb the oil.
- Serve on a plate with pesto.

Vegetables and Side Dishes

Not all of us want to eat our vegetables. But eating them makes us feel good. Make vegetables taste good and make them the way you like. All of these recipes will make you enjoy vegetables even more...
Bon Appétit!

Marie x

Stuffed Avocado

Serves 6

Ingredients

2 avocados
1 tablespoon of capers
1 onion, chopped
1 large tomato, chopped
3 tablespoons of cream cheese
Juice of one lemon
Salt and pepper to taste
Chopped fresh parsley

Preparation

- Slice the avocados in half.
- Remove the pits and carefully scoop out into a bowl. Save the avocado skins for later.
- Brush lemon juice inside skins, cover them and place in refrigerator.
- Mash / chop the avocado in a bowl. Chop the onions and tomatoes. Add to the avocados. Mix in the capers.

- Add cream cheese and the remaining lemon juice. Mix well.
- Add salt and pepper to taste, then fill each avocado skin with mixture.
- Garnish with parsley.
- Serve with tortilla chips or crackers.

Vegetables & Sides

Ratatouille

Serves 4-6

Preparation

· Wash the vegetables, cut the eggplant and zucchini into cubes.
· Dice the peppers, onions and tomatoes into small pieces.
· Heat the oil in a pan and fry the onion and garlic for 10 minutes.
· Add the zucchini and eggplant, then the tomatoes and herbs.
· Cover and simmer over low heat for 20 minutes.
· If you see that the ratatouille is a bit dry, add a little water.
· Ratatouille is a dish of southern France and can be eaten hot or cold.

Ingredients

350 grams of eggplant
350 grams of zucchini
350 grams red and green pepper
350 grams of onions
500 grams of tomatoes
3 cloves garlic, crushed
6 tablespoons of olive oil
1 sprig fresh thyme
2-3 bay leaves
Salt and pepper to taste

Gratin de Dauphinois

Serves 4-6

Ingredients

800 grams of potatoes
300 ml of whole milk
50 ml of crème fraiche
Salt and pepper
Nutmeg
Pat of butter
2 garlic cloves, crushed
Parmesan cheese, grated (for the topping)

Preparation

- Pre-heat the oven to 350 °F.
- Wash and peel the potatoes.
- Slice them and put them in a pan with the milk, cream, a little butter and seasoning.
- Bring to a boil, then reduce the heat and simmer for about 8 minutes.
- Remove from the heat and arrange the partly boiled potatoes in a flan dish, covering them with the milk and cream sauce and adding a little extra butter.
- Sprinkle with Parmesan cheese and bake for 15-20 minutes until potatoes are cooked through and the top has turned golden brown.
- Allow to cool a little and serve.

Vegetables & Sides

Green Apple and Potato Gratin

Serves 4

Preparation

- Pre-heat the oven to 350 °F.
- In a bowl, mix the cream, milk, garlic and sour cream, add seasoning. Beat in the eggs.
- Peel the potatoes and green apples, cut into slices and layer in a buttered heat proof dish.
- Pour the milk and egg mixture over this.
- Sprinkle with the cheese and bake for 45 minutes or until top is golden brown.

Ingredients

1kg of potatoes
3 green apples
200 ml crème fraiche
20 ml of milk
100 grams of shredded Swiss cheese
2 eggs
Salt and pepper
1/2 tablespoon butter/2 tablespoon of herbs de provence

Tomatoes Provençale

Serves 6

Ingredients

3 beautiful ripe tomatoes
3 cloves of garlic, chopped
3 tablespoons of parsley, chopped
3 tablespoons of basil, chopped
½ tablespoon of herbs de Provence
2 tablespoon of olive oil
Salt and pepper
Water

Preparation

· Pre-heat the oven to 350 °F.
· Cut the tomatoes in half and score the flat side.
· Place on a baking dish.
· Sprinkle with salt and pepper, crushed garlic and herbs.
· Drizzle with the olive oil.
· Pour a little water on the bottom of the pan.
· Bake 30-40 minutes.
· Serve on top of hot pasta with a little extra fresh chopped basil.

Vegetables & Sides

Eggplant Gratin

Serves 6

Preparation

- Pre-heat the oven to 375 °F.
- Slice the eggplant.
- Heat a little oil in a pan and sauté the onion. Add the eggplant with a little water and mix in the garlic, seasoning and herbs.
- Cook for 30 minutes on medium heat.
- Stir in the tomato concentrate and sauce.
- Add the Parmesan.
- Remove from the heat and layer the eggplant with the Gruyère in an oven-safe dish.
- Place in the oven and cook until the eggplant is well browned.
  Serve hot.

Ingredients

4 large eggplants
150 grams of grated Parmesan cheese
100 grams of tomato concentrate
20 grams of fresh tomato sauce
300 grams of grated Gruyère cheese
2 onions, chopped fine
2 cloves of garlic, crushed
4 tablespoons of olive oil
3 teaspoons of herbs de Provence
Salt and pepper

Papaya Gratin

Serves 4

Ingredients

4 papayas (not too ripe)
3 cloves of garlic, crushed
1 onion, chopped
1 tablespoon of flour
3 tablespoons of vegetable oil
1 egg
2 tablespoons of grated Gruyère cheese

Preparation

· Pre-heat the oven to 350 °F.
· Peel the papaya. Cut in half and take out the seeds. Cut into slices and boil for 15-20 minutes. Once cooked, mash with fork to purée.
· Heat the oil. Sauté onions and garlic until translucent. Add the flour to make a rue sauce, stirring well to avoid lumps. Add the papaya.
· Take off the heat and mix well. It should be a similar consistency to mashed potato.
· Pour the gratin mixture into a greased baking dish.
· Sprinkle with cheese and place in the oven for 30 minutes or until slightly browned.

Vegetables & Sides

Cauliflower Gratin

Serves 4-6

Preparation

- Pre-heat the oven to 350 °F.
- Separate the cauliflower into florets and wash in vinegar and water.
- Put in a pan of salted water and cook for 20 minutes.
- Meanwhile, prepare the béchamel: Melt butter and add flour while stirring.
- Add cold milk and continue to stir until it has thickened.
- Add salt and pepper and a pinch of nutmeg.
- Cut the cheese into small cubes and add to the béchamel sauce.
- Drain the cauliflower and place in a buttered dish.
- Cover with the béchamel sauce and season.
- Sprinkle with a little extra grated cheese.
- Bake for 10 minutes until golden.
- Serve hot. Beautiful!

Ingredients

1 kg of cauliflower
150 grams of cheese
A pinch of nutmeg
50 grams of butter
30 grams of flour
Salt and pepper
White vinegar

Basic béchamel:
60 grams of butter
4 tablespoons of flour
900 ml of milk
Pinch of salt
Pinch of nutmeg

Chayote Gratin

Serves 6

Ingredients

4 chayotes
300 grams of chopped bacon
300 grams of grated Parmesan
150 grams of bread crumbs
3 tablespoons of olive oil
3 onions, chopped
1 small chili pepper
3 tablespoons of chopped parsley
1 small carton of sour cream
2 tablespoons of flour
35 grams of butter
300 ml of milk
Salt and pepper

Preparation

· Pre-heat the oven to 350 °F.
· Cut the chayotes in half and boil them for 20 minutes.
· Heat the oil in a pan and sauté the onions and bacon until golden brown.
· Add the herbs and allow to simmer on a low heat.
· Drain the chayotes, peel and remove the core and cut into slices. Add to the onion mix.
· Add the flour, cheese and sour cream. Season to taste.
· Butter a baking dish and arrange the chayote mix, topping it with the cheese.
· Bake in the oven for 10-15 minutes until crispy and brown on top.
· Serve hot.

Vegetables & Sides

Indian Chick Peas

Preparation

- Boil the potatoes until tender. Drain and set aside.
- Heat oil and sauté onions and jalapeño for 5 minutes.
- Add garlic and ginger. Cook until onions are soft.
- Add the tomatoes, turmeric and curry powder. Cook for 1-2 minutes more.
- Add potatoes and chick peas. Stir in the fenugreek. Add one cup of water. Add salt to taste. Cover and simmer for 10 minutes.
- Put into a bowl and garnish with fresh cilantro when ready to serve.

Ingredients

300 grams of potatoes, peeled and cut into 1 inch cubes
500 grams of chick peas, cooked or canned
2 tablespoons of olive oil
1 large onion, chopped
1 garlic clove, crushed
1 level teaspoon of fresh grated ginger
1 tomato, chopped
1 small jalapeño, chopped
1 tablespoon of fresh chopped cilantro
1 teaspoon of fenugreek
1 teaspoon of yellow curry powder
Pinch turmeric
Salt to taste

Rice with Carrots

Serves 4-6

Ingredients

1 large onion, chopped
3 large carrots, grated
400 grams of long grain rice
½ teaspoon of saffron
2 tablespoons of olive oil
1 litre chicken stock
100 ml of white wine

Preparation

· Sauté the onions in 2 tablespoons of olive oil.
· Add the carrots and rice, and stir.
· Add the white wine and stock, plus the spice and seasoning.
· Cook for 20 minutes until the water is absorbed.
· Serve hot or cold.

Vegetables & Sides

Mango Rice

Serves 4-6

Preparation

- Rinse the rice and cook in a pan with the coconut milk and water.
- Cook until the water has been absorbed.
- In a wok, add onions, curry paste and stir well.
- Add the rice and cook for 10 minutes.
- Add the mango and coriander then serve.

Ingredients

200 grams of Thai rice
200 ml of coconut milk plus a little water
1 onion, finely chopped
1 tablespoon of red curry paste
1 ripe mango, diced
A handful of chopped coriander

Risotto with Summer Vegetables

Serves 4-6

Ingredients

300 grams of risotto rice
1 onion, chopped
1 zucchini, chopped
1 eggplant, chopped
1 tomato, chopped
2 cloves garlic, crushed
60 grams of Parmesan
1 litre of chicken broth
125 ml white wine
2 tablespoons of olive oil
Chopped basil

Preparation

· Heat the oil in a pan and add the onion. Sauté until brown.
· Add the vegetables.
· Add the rice and stir until it becomes translucent.
· Add the wine and stir until it evaporates, then begin to ladle in the broth a little at a time.
· Wait until the previous ladle has been absorbed before adding the next one.
· When all the broth has been used and the rice is cooked and creamy, add the Parmesan and serve.
· So simple. So tasty!

Vegetables & Sides

Cumin Rice

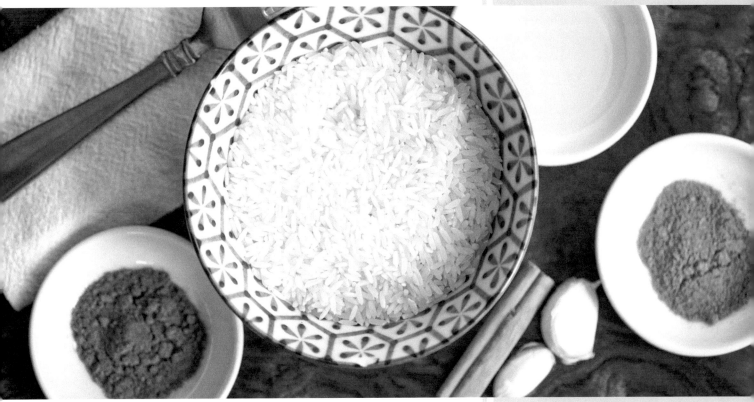

Serves 4

Preparation

- In a wok, heat the butter and oil, add the the spices and fry 3 to 4 minutes.
- Add the rice and the water and bring to a boil.
- Season and reduce the heat to a simmer.
- Cook for 20 minutes or until the water has been absorbed.

Ingredients

3 cups basmati rice
1 clove garlic, crushed
60 grams of butter
1 tablespoon of olive oil
1 small cinnamon stick
1 star anise
2 tablespoons of cumin
2 tablespoons of garam masala
Salt and pepper
Water

Salads

Beautiful salads that complement my dressings perfectly.

Marie x

Carrot, Beet and Coconut Salad

Serves 6

Preparation

· Toss together all ingredients. Spoon into 6 cups or drinking glasses.
· Refrigerate and serve with a lemon wedge.

Ingredients

3 carrots, grated
2 raw beets, grated
1 small fresh coconut shredded or 2 cups pre-shredded unsweetened dried coconut
3 green onions, finely chopped
Mint, chopped
Cilantro, chopped
Juice of one lemon
Juice and zest of one orange
4 tablespoons of olive oil
Salt, pepper, and/or chili flakes to taste

Tunisian Carrot Salad

Serves 6

Ingredients

500 grams carrots
3 tablespoons (or a bunch) of finely chopped parsley
1 teaspoon ground cumin
5 tablespoons olive oil
4 tablespoons red wine vinegar
2 cloves garlic, crushed
½ teaspoon Harissa (Harissa is a purée of red peppers, season to taste)
12 black olives
2 boiled eggs, quartered
Salt and freshly ground pepper
3 cups of water

Preparation

· Cut carrots into thin rounds.
· In a saucepan, boil 3 cups of water, then add the sliced carrots and cook until tender.
· Strain and pour into a bowl.
· Stir in parsley, cumin, olive oil, vinegar and garlic.
· Season to your taste with Harissa, salt, pepper, then mix.
· Put the salad in a serving dish and garnish with the olives and hard-boiled egg quarters.

Salad d'Avocat

Serves 6

Preparation

- Mix avocados, onion, tomato and lime juice.
- In a separate container, mix remaining ingredients for the dressing.
- Add the dressing to the avocado mixture.
- Refrigerate/chill until you are ready to serve.

Ingredients

2 large avocados sliced into cubes

1 minced red onion

1 tablespoon of lime juice

1 diced tomato

1 diced small red pepper

1 teaspoon of coriander

1 teaspoon of cumin

3 tablespoons of fresh chopped cilantro

2 tablespoons of olive oil

4-5 drops Tabasco

Tofu Salad

Serves 4

Ingredients

2 teaspoons of Thai chili sauce
½ teaspoon of fresh grated ginger
1 garlic clove, crushed
2 teaspoons of soy sauce
2 tablespoons of vegetable oil
250 grams of tofu
100 grams of pea pods
2 small carrots, chopped
100 grams of red cabbage, shredded fine
2 tablespoons of chopped peanuts

Preparation

· Mix the chili sauce, ginger, pressed garlic and soy sauce.
· Cut the tofu into 2 cm cubes. Put into a bowl and pour sauce over, gently mixing. Cover and refrigerate for 1 hour.
· Cut the pea pods into 3 cm pieces. Place pea pods in boiling water for 2 minutes. Remove and rinse with cold water.
· Cut carrots into matchsticks and thinly slice cabbage.

· Place vegetables in bowl with the marinating tofu and mix.
· Refrigerate until ready to serve.
· Garnish with peanuts.
  So simple, so delicious!

Salads

Potato Salad with Egg, Avocado and Red Onion

Serves 4

Preparation

· Boil the potatoes with the skin on for 10
  minutes, cool and slice.
· Hard boil the eggs, allow to cool, peel and
  slice.
· Arrange both in a bowl with the avocado,
  olives and onion.
· Make a dressing with the oil, vinegar, herbs,
  lemon juice and seasoning.
· Mix it well and pour over the salad.
  Bon appétit!

Ingredients

6 small potatoes
3 boiled eggs
1 large red onion, sliced thin
2 avocados, sliced
12 black olives, pitted
4 tablespoons of dry white wine
4 tablespoons of olive oil
2 teaspoons of tarragon
1 tablespoon of mustard
1 lemon, juiced
Salt and pepper to taste

Beet and Orange Salad

Serves 4

Ingredients

300 grams of cooked beetroot
1 orange, peeled and sliced
1 bunch mint, chopped
For the Vinaigrette
1 orange, juiced
1 tablespoon of cumin seed
1 tablespoon of mustard
1 tablespoon of wine vinegar (white or red)
3 tablespoons of olive oil
Salt and pepper

Preparation

· Cut the beets into small 2 cm cubes.
· Peel the orange and cut into slices, removing any white pith.
· Chop the mint and combine all ingredients together in a bowl.
· For the vinaigrette, mix everything together in a small mixing bowl and stir well.
· Pour the vinaigrette over the ingredients and chill for 1 hour.
· Serve with pita bread.

Salads

Salad Niçoise

Serves 4

Preparation

- Wash and prepare all the vegetables. Add them to a bowl.
- Cook the beans until tender and add those too.
- Arrange the sliced eggs, tuna, anchovies and olives nicely.
- Make a dressing with the olive oil and lemon juice.
- Season to taste.
- Drizzle the salad with dressing.

Ingredients

200 grams of mesclun / mixed salad
4 small tomatoes, chopped
150 grams of tuna in brine
8 small white onions, sliced
200 grams of green beans
1 red pepper, sliced
4 hard-boiled eggs, sliced
1 small jar of anchovies
100 grams of black olives, pitted

For the Dressing:
A few basil leaves, chopped
1 lemon, juiced
Olive oil
Salt and pepper

Serves 4

Ingredients

1 cup of green lentils
¼ red cabbage, shredded
1 bunch of tarragon, chopped
1 large red onion, chopped
1 small bunch of thyme, chopped
4 bay leaves
2 or 3 parsley stalks
4 small tomatoes, chopped
2 cups of water

For the dressing:
6 to 7 tbsp of olive oil
3 tbsp of cider vinegar
1 tbsp of liquid honey
Salt and pepper

Preparation

· Put the lentils in a saucepan and cover with 2 glasses of water. Add thyme & parsley sprigs with a little salt and pepper and boil for 20 minutes.
· Remove the core of the cabbage and shred the leaves.
· Wash and dry the grapes and cut into halves.
· Cut the tomatoes into small wedges, then combine all ingredients together: lentils, cabbage, grapes, tomatoes and stir.

· Prepare the dressing by mixing all ingredients together, add the remaining herbs.
· Pour over the salad mix and marinate for 30 minutes at room temperature first, then place in the fridge for 20 minutes to chill before serving.

Salads

Mango Salad

Serves 4

Preparation

· Place the mango cubes into a serving bowl.
· In a separate bowl, whisk together the lemon, oil, spices and herbs.
· Season to taste.
· When well mixed, pour over the mango and place in the refrigerator for 20 minutes.
· You can also add some avocado slices if you'd like.
  Heavenly.

Ingredients

4 medium mangoes, cubed
1 cup of lemon juice
2 tablespoons of olive oil
1 tablespoon of red pepper flakes
2 tablespoons of fresh cilantro, chopped
2 tablespoons of shallots, chopped
Salt and black pepper to season
4 avocado slices (optional)
1 tablespoon of french mustard

Salad Dressing

There cannot be a good salad without a good salad dressing - it's like food without a good wine.

Marie x

Passion Fruit Dressing

Serves 6

Preparation

- This is so simple. Just mix everything together in a bowl... and your dressing is ready.

Ingredients

1 passion fruit, scoop out the flesh
2 tablespoons of mayonnaise
2 tablespoons of olive oil
1 tablespoon of white wine
Salt and pepper to taste

French Dressing

Serves 6

Ingredients

2 garlic cloves, minced
1 tablespoon of honey
1 tablespoon of lemon juice
1 tablespoon of French mustard
3 tablespoons of olive oil

Preparation

· Mix all the ingredients together, whisking vigorously.
Bon appétit!

Salad Dressing

Tomato Vinaigrette

Preparation

· Mix all ingredients in a jar.
· Shake vigorously.

Ingredients

5 large tomatoes
1 tablespoon of mustard
5 tablespoons of olive oil
2 tablespoons of red wine vinegar
A pinch of sugar
Salt and pepper

Chocolate Dressing

Serves 6

Ingredients

2 tablespoons of balsamic vinegar
2 tablespoons of rice wine vinegar or white vinegar
30 grams of dark chocolate, melted
2 tablespoons of water
4-5 tablespoons of olive oil
Salt and ground pepper to season

Preparation

· Combine ingredients in a bowl and mix well.

Orange and Basil Vinaigrette

Serves 6

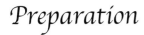

Preparation

· Combine the ingredients in a blender or food processor.

Ingredients

1 tablespoon of olive oil
1 teaspoon of nut oil
2 teaspoons of mustard
Salt and pepper
1 tablespoon of white vinegar
1 teaspoon of soy sauce
3 oranges, juiced
A small handful of fresh basil, chopped

Zesty Dressing

Serves 6

Ingredients

4 tablespoons of olive oil
4 tablespoons of canola oil
½ cup of apple or rice vinegar
2 fresh tomatoes, cut into quarters
1 medium green apple, sliced into quarters
2 tablespoons of sugar
½ teaspoon of salt
1 teaspoon of tomato paste
¼ teaspoon of paprika
1 garlic clove, crushed

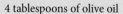 Preparation

· Mix everything in the blender and serve.

Salad Dressing

Soups

Hot or cold... there is nothing better to start a meal than soup. Let us take you on an exploration of the world through soup - Indian lentil soup or spinach soup with curry, French onion soup, Maroccan chickpea soup, Spanish tomato, mint and cucumber gazpacho - for example, all of them delicious! Soups that the whole family will love.

Marie x

Cream of Cauliflower Soup

Serves 4-6

Ingredients

2 beautiful cauliflowers
1 litre of water
Salt and pepper
A handful of chopped parsley
Butter for frying

Preparation

· Remove the leaves from the cauliflower, chop into florets and wash.
· Keep the leaves.
· Bring the water to a boil in a large pan on high heat, add the cauliflower and cook for 20 minutes.
· Meanwhile, sauté the leaves in a little butter and seasoning for 5 minutes.
· Add the leaves into the pan with the cauliflower florets and blend together with a hand blender.
· To serve, sprinkle with chopped parsley and season to taste.

Coconut Milk Thai Chicken Soup

Serves 4-6

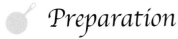 ## Preparation

- Cut the chicken into small pieces.
- Peel and chop the onion, cut the mushrooms and sprinkle with lime juice then add the basil.
- Heat the oil in a wok and add the chicken, frying for 5-6 minutes. Remove from pan and put to one side.
- Sauté the onion until soft and then add a little water.

- Add the corn, mushrooms and all remaining ingredients, including the coconut milk.
- Season and simmer for a few minutes to allow the flavors to infuse.
- Add the chicken and bring to a boil, cook for 10 -15 minutes and serve immediately.

Ingredients

4 chicken breasts, cut into chunks
500 ml coconut milk
125 grams of corn kernels
4 mushrooms
1 tablespoon of olive oil
2 limes, juiced
1 tablespoon of ginger, grated
1 large onion, chopped
1 teaspoon of curry powder
1 teaspoon of chili powder
3 sticks of lemon grass
1 small bunch of basil, chopped
Salt and pepper

'Shu'Bah' - Indian Tomato Soup

Serves 4-6

Ingredients

800 grams of tomatoes cut into quarters
80 grams of white onions, chopped
One small cinnamon stick
3 green cardamom seeds
2 cloves of garlic, crushed
1 tablespoon of fresh ginger, grated
1 teaspoon of turmeric or cumin
1 teaspoon of chili powder
1 teaspoon of thyme
3 tablespoons of ghee (clarified butter)/
butter or olive oil if ghee isn't available
Salt and pepper to season

Preparation

- Heat ghee or oil in a saucepan on medium heat.
- Add the spices, cinnamon, cardamom and cloves and stir, gently cooking for 5 minutes to infuse flavors.
- Add the onion, garlic, ginger and stir.
- Add the tomatoes and just enough water to cover. Simmer until soft then add the remaining spices. Add a little more water if needed and continue to cook for 20 minutes.
- Season to taste and serve.

Soups

Cream of Zucchini with Fresh Mint

Serves 4-6

Preparation

· Peel and coarsely chop the onion.
· Cut the zucchinis into rounds.
· Cut the potatoes into cubes.
· Heat the oil in a pan and sauté the onion until soft.
· Add the water and bring to a boil. Then add the potatoes.
· Add the vegetable stock cube and simmer for 15 minutes.
· Add the zucchini and mint.
· Continue cooking 10 minutes more and blend with a hand blender.
· Season with salt and pepper and serve with slices of grilled country bread.

Ingredients

1 large onion
700 grams of zucchini
1 large potato
500 ml of water
1 cube of vegetable broth
1 tablespoon of olive oil
A handful of fresh mint, chopped
Salt and pepper

Carrot Soup with Ginger, Orange and Cumin

Serves 4-6

Ingredients

1 kg of carrots
1 orange, juiced and zested
1 litre of vegetable broth or water
150 grams of crème fraiche
4 tablespoons of olive oil
2 teaspoons of ground cumin
1 sprig of fresh rosemary, chopped
1 small handful of fresh cilantro, chopped
Salt and freshly ground pepper

Preparation

· Peel carrots and chop.
· Juice and zest the orange.
· Chop the herbs finely.
· Heat the broth in a pot, add the carrots, herbs, orange juice, zest, ginger, cumin and a little seasoning.
· Simmer on low heat for 30-40 minutes.
· Add the oil and the crème fraiche, then blend.
· Serve hot or cold.

Spinach Lentil Soup

Serves 4-6

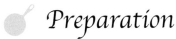 ## Preparation

- Wash lentils, drain and set aside.
- Prepare the vegetables: finely chop the onions, carrots and celery. Mince the garlic and grate the ginger. Set aside.
- Heat the oil in a pan and sauté the vegetables 8 to 10 minutes until everything is golden brown.
- Add the curry powder, ginger, cumin and bay leaf. Cook and stir for 1 minute. Then add the water and lentils.
- Bring to a boil and simmer on medium heat for 30 minutes. Then add the spinach and cook 5 minutes longer.
- Season with salt and pepper and remove the bay leaf before serving.
- Serve with a bowl of cooling yoghurt on the side.

Ingredients

400 grams of lentils, cooked
1 onion, finely chopped
1 carrot, cut into thin strips
1 stick of celery, chopped
2 cloves garlic, minced
1 tablespoon of fresh ginger, grated
2 tablespoons of olive oil
1 teaspoon of curry powder
1 teaspoon of cumin
1 bay leaf
2 litres of water
170 grams of spinach
Salt and pepper to taste

Basil Tomato Soup

Serves 4

Ingredients

6 large tomatoes, peeled and chopped
1 potato, chopped
1 onion, sliced
2 cloves garlic, minced
3 tablespoons of sour cream
A few basil leaves, chopped
500 ml of water or chicken stock
2 tablespoons of olive oil
Salt and pepper to season

Preparation

- Fill a pan with water and bring to a boil. Dip the tomatoes in for 10 seconds, drain and refresh under cold water so the skin is easy to remove.
- Cut the tomatoes and set aside.
- Prepare the vegetables.
- Pour olive oil in a pan. Sauté onions and garlic, stir well.
- When the onion becomes transparent, add the tomato pieces, stir in the potatoes and add salt to season.
- Simmer for 30 minutes until the vegetables are cooked through.
- Blend with a hand blender, add sour cream and garnish with basil leaf to serve.

French Onion Soup

 ## Preparation

- Slice the onions very fine. In a heavy bottomed pan heat the oil and butter.
- Sauté the onion and garlic until translucent.
- Add the flour, the broth, the wine and seasoning.
- Bring to a boil then simmer on a reduced heat for 40 minutes.
- Serve with croutons and grated Gruyère cheese!

Ingredients

½ kg of onions (about 5 medium onions)
2 garlic cloves, minced
2 tablespoons of olive oil
50 grams of butter
2 litres of vegetarian or beef broth
1 ½ glasses of white wine
1 tablespoon of flour
Salt and pepper to season
1 tablespoon of soy sauce…
my secret ingredient

Papaya Gazpacho

Serves 4

Ingredients

2 ripe papayas, cut into chunks,
seeds removed
½ pineapple, cubed
Cold water
4 mint leaves
1 tablespoon of fresh ginger, grated
1 glass of white wine
2 lemons, juiced
1 cup of coconut milk
Sugar if needed
Mint leaves to garnish

Preparation

· Blend the first 5 ingredients and strain.
· Put the mixture in a pan over a medium
  heat and add the wine, lemon juice, coconut
  milk and a little sugar, if using.
· Remove from the heat, strain again and
  allow to cool.
· Serve with mint leaves.

Green Gazpacho

 ## Preparation

- Cut the vegetables and place them in a food processor with the lemon juice, olive oil, herbs and Tabasco sauce.
- Mix everything finely, adding a little water at a time until you achieve the desired consistency.
- Chill and serve.

Ingredients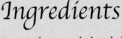

2 cucumbers, peeled and chopped
5 green apples, peeled and chopped
4 small white onions, chopped
1 lemon, juiced
4-5 tablespoons of olive oil
8 sprigs fresh cilantro, chopped
2 sprigs basil, chopped
½ teaspoon of Tabasco sauce
Salt and pepper

Watermelon Gazpacho with Tomato and Basil

Serves 4

Ingredients

¼ of large watermelon cut away from rind and chopped
3 tomatoes, peeled and de-seeded
1 red pepper, chopped fine
1 large onion
2 cloves garlic
2 tablespoons of paprika
A pinch of cumin
2 tablespoons of olive oil
4 tablespoons of wine vinegar
4 tablespoons of tomato juice or water
A little Tabasco sauce

Preparation

· Mix all ingredients (except the bread) in a food processor and pass the soup through a sieve to strain.
· Chill and serve with the following accompaniments:
croutons, toasted slivered almonds, a little chopped basil and grated cucumber
(if desired).

Soups

Desserts

The dessert is "la cerise sur le gateau" a French expression that can not be translated. But let me try: it means "the cherry topping the cake." After a delicious meal, what better way to be sent to your dreams than a "la touche de chef" - the final touch!!

Marie x

Basic Crêpes Recipe

Serves 8-10

Ingredients

250 grams of flour

4 eggs

750 ml milk

100 grams sugar (omit if making savory crêpes)

A pinch of salt

4 teaspoons of oil

½ cup of water

½ packet of vanilla sugar

You can add 1 teaspoon of dark rum
(sweet only) if you like

Butter for frying

Preparation

- Place the flour in a bowl, make a well and break the eggs in one-by-one. Stir slowly, mixing in a little flour at a time.
- When the mixture has thickened, pour in the milk slowly, avoiding lumps. Add salt, sugar, oil and water.
- Beat with a whisk and let rest 2 hours.
- Heat a frying pan over medium heat.
- Pour the batter into the pan using approximately ¼ cup for each crêpe.
- Cook for 1-2 minutes until the bottom turns golden brown, then turn it over and cook the other side.
- Serve hot.
- Spread warm crêpes with Nutella, fold them and sprinkle with powdered sugar for a chocolaty treat.

Crêpes Suzette

 ## Preparation

- Make the crêpe batter and cook the crêpes.
- Juice the oranges and lemons.
- Sprinkle the powdered sugar on the bottom of a hot frying pan and add a little butter.
- When it begins to caramelize, add the juice of lemons and oranges, then flambé the Grand Marnier and remove from the heat.
- Dip the pancakes one at a time into this mixture, covering both sides.
- Fold them in two and dip them into the mixture again to soak up the juice.
- Arrange the Crêpes Suzette on a plate and drizzle with the juice. Serve hot.

Ingredients

1 batch of basic crêpe batter
2 oranges, juiced
2 lemons, juiced
1-2 tablespoons of sugar
125 ml of Grand Marnier
Butter for frying

Mango Mousse

Serves 4

Ingredients

1 ripe mango
200 ml of crème fraiche, whipped
Juice and zest of 1 orange
3 eggs
5 tablespoons of sugar
3 tablespoons of powdered sugar

Preparation

· Peel mango and cut into small pieces or purée.
· Heat a small pan and add the mango, orange juice and 2 tablespoons of sugar. Cook over low heat and gently bring to a boil for 15 minutes or until the sugar has dissolved and the mixture is syrupy and thick.
· Meanwhile, take the eggs and separate the whites from the yolks. Mix the yolks with 3 tablespoons of sugar until mixture is frothy, then beat the egg whites until very firm.
· Gradually add the hot mango sugar into the egg whites until the mixture is gelatinous.
· Fold in the crème fraiche, orange zest and powdered sugar (if needed) and mix well. Place in the refrigerator to cool for 2 hours. To serve, place the mousse in small glass jars.

Mango Cheesecake

Serves 6-8

 ## Preparation

- Pre-heat the oven to 250 °F.
- Crush the cookies and mix in a bowl with the butter.
- Grease the bottom of a flan dish or cheesecake mold with a loose base, line the bottom with the cookie base mixture and chill.
- In a bowl, mix the cream cheese, sugar, flour and fresh cream until smooth.
- Pour the mixture into the mold and place in a hot oven.
- After 15 minutes, reduce the oven temperature and bake for 20 minutes further or until a cake tester (or knife tip) comes away clean.
- Peel and cut the mango into thin strips and arrange them on the cheesecake. Allow to cool and serve.

Ingredients

250 grams of butter cookies
500 grams of Philadelphia cream cheese
150 grams of sugar
60 grams of soft butter, melted
50 grams of flour
3 eggs
50 grams heavy cream
2 mangoes
A few poppy seeds and fresh mint leaves

Tangine de Fruits

Serves 6

Ingredients

1 lime, juiced and zested
2 oranges, juiced
100 grams of raisins
2 tablespoons of honey
1 teaspoon of cinnamon
1 teaspoon of powdered ginger
1 teaspoon of vanilla
3 mangoes, chopped
2 apples, peeled & chopped
2 pears, peeled & chopped
1 cup whole dried figs
2 cloves
2 tablespoons of roasted slivered almonds
Fresh mint

Preparation

· You will need a tagine dish.
· Pre-heat the oven to a medium heat.
· Zest and juice the lime.
· Juice the oranges separately.
· In a bowl, pour the juice of one orange and add the raisins.
· Let this rest for 1 hour.
· Put the juice of the second orange in a small pan over a gentle heat and add the lime juice, honey, cinnamon, ginger, vanilla, and cloves. Cook for 10 minutes until flavors have combined. Set aside.

· Peel the apples and pears then core and slice. Peel and cut the mango into strips.
· Place the fruit in the tagine and top with halved figs.
· Pour honey sauce over the fruit, cover and cook in the oven for 15 minutes. Add the raisins and lime juice.
· Gently mix and let cook another 15 minutes.
· Serve in the tagine.
· Garnish with grilled almonds and mint. Just incredible!

Desserts

Star Fruit Tart

Serves 6-8

 ## Preparation

- Preheat oven to 350 °F.
- Arrange sliced star fruit in the bottom of a greased 9-inch cake tin as close together as possible.
- Mix together the softened butter, brown sugar and passion fruit juice and pour into pan so mixture covers bottom. Set aside.
- Cream together the rest of the butter and sugar. Add the eggs, one at a time and beat well.
- Mix together the dry ingredients in a separate bowl.
- Add everything together a little at a time. Slowly add the milk, stirring continuously so it doesn't become lumpy.
- Stir in vanilla and almond extracts, then pour into the prepared cake tin.
- Bake for approximately 30 minutes or until cake pulls away from sides of pan.
- Let cool for five minutes before inverting onto a serving plate.

Ingredients

3 to 4 star fruit, sliced
113 grams of butter, softened
75 grams of butter, melted
1 cup of sugar
150 grams of dark brown sugar
200 grams of cake flour
1 ½ teaspoons baking powder
2 eggs
120 ml of whole milk
Juice of 1 passion fruit
1 teaspoon pure vanilla extract
1 teaspoon pure almond extract
Sea salt

Chocolate Mousse

Serves 4

Ingredients

50 grams of dark chocolate
50 grams of milk chocolate
3 eggs
A pinch of salt

Preparation

· Melt the chocolate in a double boiler.
· Separate the eggs and pour the yolks into the chocolate and whisk well.
· In a separate bowl beat the egg whites until stiff with a pinch of salt.
· Once the whites are firm and shiny, fold gently into the chocolate mixture until fully mixed.
· Refrigerate for 2 hours.
· Serve in individual ramekins, if desired.

Desserts

Lemon Meringue Pie

Preparation

- Pre-heat the oven to 350 °F.
- Grease a pie pan with a loose bottom, if available.
- Mix the cookies in a food processor with 30 grams of the butter.
- Spread the mix into the base of the pie pan and press down, forming a crust. Set aside.
- Mix together the cornstarch with 100 grams of sugar, the water and lemon juice. Place in a small pan and bring to a boil over a medium heat, stirring constantly to prevent burning.
- Remove from the heat and add 60 grams of cubed butter, stir well and allow to cool for 20 minutes.
- Pour the lemon mixture into the pan with the cookie crust and put it in the refrigerator for 2 hours.
- Beat the egg whites until very firm while adding, little by little, the remaining sugar and lemon zest.
- Pour this into the pie pan , on top of the lemon mixture, bringing the egg whites into small peaks.
- Place in the oven for 5-6 minutes until lightly browned.

Ingredients

250 grams of butter cookies, for pie crust
100 grams of butter, softened
75 grams of cornstarch
350 grams powdered sugar
125 ml lemon juice
60 grams butter in cubes
4 eggs (yolks and whites separated)
1 tablespoon of lemon juice and lemon zest
300ml water

Chocolate Cake with Passion Fruit

Serves 4

Ingredients

175 grams of dark chocolate
100 grams of sugar
100 grams of butter
30 grams of flour
2 eggs
2 passion fruit
Optional: 100 grams of powdered almonds

Preparation

- Pre-heat the oven to 350 °F.
- Melt the chocolate and butter in a Bain Marie over a gentle heat.
- Scoop out the passion fruit flesh and filter through a sieve to remove the seeds.
- Remove from the heat and beat in the eggs, flour, sugar and the flesh of the passion fruit (plus the almonds, if using).
- Mix well and pour the mixture into a greased brownie tray.
- Place in the oven for 20 minutes or until a cake tester comes away clean.
- Serve with custard.

Almond Macaroons

Serves 6-12

 ## Preparation

- Pre-heat the oven to 350 °F.
- Mix the almonds, the vanilla extract and sugar in a bowl.
- Break eggs, separate whites from yolks.
- Pour the whites into the mix and beat well with an electric mixer.
- Spread a sheet of parchment paper on a baking tray.
- Spoon rounds of batter onto the tray with plenty of space between each one.
- Bake in the oven for 20 minutes.
- Allow to cool before serving.

Ingredients

250 grams of powdered almonds
200grams of caster sugar
4 eggs
1 tablespoon of vanilla extract

Banana Mousse

Serves 8

Ingredients

3 bananas
3 egg whites
2 tablespoons icing sugar
3 tablespoons of brown sugar
1 tablespoon of fresh lemon juice
2 cups of Chantilly cream
1 teaspoon of cinnamon

Preparation

· Mash the banana to a purée, pour over the lemon juice and mix together in a bowl.
· Fold in the cinnamon and brown sugar. Stir.
· Mix in the Chantilly cream.
· Whisk the egg whites until they make firm peaks, then fold in the icing sugar.
· Mix this together with the banana mixture.
· Decant in individual glasses to serve and place in the fridge to set for 2 hours.
· Serve with banana cookies. Delicious.

Desserts

Beverages

Every meal has its drink - for waking up in the morning, a good natural juice; for lunch, a smoothie with mixed fruit, herbs and vegetables; and before dinner, a nice cocktail to be enjoyed. This is my way to fully appreciate all the recipes of this book, which I crafted with love and appreciation.

Marie x

Lemon Ginger Tea

Makes 1 Liter

Ingredients

50 grams of fresh ginger, grated
1 litre of water
2 limes, juiced
2-3 teaspoons of brown sugar
½ teaspoon of cinnamon,
1 clove

Preparation

· Put all the ingredients in a pan and bring
  to a boil.
· Then turn off heat, cover and allow to sit for
  1 hour.
· Filter into a decanter and serve chilled.

Banana, Mango, Ginger, Orange Smoothie

Serves 2

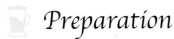

Preparation

· Cut mango into cubes removing the pit and skin.
· Chop the banana.
· Juice the oranges.
· Combine everything into a blender, including the ginger and yoghurt.
· Blend until smooth and creamy, adding a little water if needed.
· Add a dozen ice cubes and blend once more.
· Serve in tall glasses decorated with a slice of lime.

Ingredients

1 mango
1-2 bananas
2 oranges, juiced
200 ml of plain yoghurt
A pinch of ginger powder
12 ice cubes
2 slices of lime

Orange Juice, Banana, Pineapple and Passion Fruit Smoothie

Serves 2

Ingredients

4 slices ripe pineapple, cubed
1 orange, juiced
1 banana, chopped
1 passion fruit
½ lime, juiced
1 cup of water

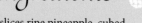 Preparation

· Put the pineapple, orange juice, banana, passion fruit and lime juice in a blender with a cup of water and blend together until smooth.
· Strain before serving to remove the passion fruit seeds.
· Serve over ice in tall glasses.

Massala Chai

Preparation

- Bring the water to a boil in a pot.
- Add the spices and the tea.
- Stir in the sugar and remove from the heat.
- Strain liquid (tea) into a bowl or pot and save. (compost/discard tea leaves and spices)
- Heat the milk separately, then add liquid tea and stir. Serve hot in coffee /tea mugs. Garnish with cinnamon.

Ingredients

5 cardamom pods
1 tablespoon of ginger, grated
1 cinnamon stick or 2 teaspoons of cinnamon powder
5 black peppercorns
6 teaspoons of sugar
4 teaspoons of loose black tea (according to taste)
2 cloves
400 ml of milk
40 ml water

Lassi

Serves 4

Ingredients

500 grams of plain yoghurt
120 ml of milk
A pinch of salt
4-5 green cardamom pods, crushed
3 drops of rose water or fruit syrup
4 mint leaves

Preparation

• Place all the ingredients into a blender and
  mix well until smooth.
• Serve in 4 20 ml glasses of ice, garnish with
  a mint leaf.

Soy-Banana Milk Shake

Preparation

- Place ingredients in a blender, process until smooth and serve.

Ingredients

80 ml of soy milk
1 banana, peeled and cut into chunks
4 ice cubes

Conversion Table

Weight

U.S.	METRIC
.035 ounce	1 gram
0.5 oz.	14 grams
1 oz.	28 grams
1/4 pound (lb)	113 grams
1/3 pound (lb)	151 grams
1/2 pound (lb)	227 grams
1 pound (lb)	454 grams
1.10 pounds (lbs)	500 grams
2.205 pounds (lbs)	1 kilogram
35 oz.	1 kilogram

Equivalents

U.S.	METRIC
16 tablespoons	1 cup
12 tablespoons	3/4 cup
10 tablespoons + 2 teaspoons	2/3 cup
8 tablespoons	1/2 cup
6 tablespoons	3/8 cup
5 tablespoons + 1 teaspoon	1/3 cup
4 tablespoons	1/4 cup
2 tablespoons + 2 teaspoons	1/6 cup
2 tablespoons	1/8 cup
1 tablespoon	1/16 cup
1 pint	2 cups
1 quart	2 pints
1 tablespoon	3 teaspoons
1 cup	48 teaspoons
1 cup	16 tablespoons

Capacity

U.S.	METRIC
1/5 teaspoon	1 ml
1 teaspoon (tsp)	5 ml
1 tablespoon (tbsp)	15 ml
1 fluid oz.	30 ml
1/5 cup	50 ml
1/4 cup	60 ml
1/3 cup	80 ml
3.4 fluid oz.	100 ml
1/2 cup	120 ml
2/3 cup	160 ml
3/4 cup	180 ml
1 cup	240 ml
1 pint (2 cups)	480 ml
1 quart (4 cups)	.95 litre
34 fluid oz.	1 litre
4.2 cups	1 litre
2.1 pints	1 litre
1.06 quarts	1 litre
.26 gallon	1 litre
4 quarts (1 gallon)	3.8 litres

Sugar

U.S.	METRIC
1 cup of caster sugar	200 grams
1 cup of raw sugar	250 grams
1 cup of brown sugar	220 grams
1 cup of confectioners(icing) sugar	125 grams
1 teaspoon of caster sugar	4.2 grams
1 tablespoon of caster sugar	12.6 grams

Yeast

U.S.	METRIC
1 teaspoon instant dry yeast	3.1 grams
2 1/4 teaspoons instant dry yeast	7 grams
1 tablespoon instant dry yeast	9.3 grams
7 grams instant dry yeast	21 grams fresh yeast

Flour

U.S.	METRIC
1 cup all-purpose flour (USDA)	125 grams
1 cup all-purpose flour (Gold Medal)	130 grams
1 cup whole wheat flour (USDA)	120 grams
1 cup whole wheat flour (Gold Medal)	128 grams
1 cup bread flour (USDA)	127 grams
1 cup bread flour (Gold Medal)	135 grams
1 cup rye flour (USDA)	102 grams
King Arthur says ALL flour types	113 grams
1 tablespoon of flour	between 8 and 9 grams

Converting Fahrenheit and Celsius

To convert Fahrenheit to Celsius, subtract 32 degrees and divide by 1.8

To convert Celsius to Fahrenheit, multiply by 1.8 and add 32 degrees

Butter

U.S.	METRIC
1 tablespoon	14.175 grams
1 stick	4 ounces
1 stick	1/2 cup
1 stick	8 tablespoons
1 stick	113 grams
1 cup	226 grams

Salt

U.S.	METRIC
1/4 teaspoon	1.42 grams
1/2 teaspoon	2.84 grams
1 teaspoon	5.69 grams
1/2 tablespoon	8.53 grams
1 tablespoon	17.07 grams

Honey

U.S.	METRIC
1 tablespoon	21.25 grams
1/4 cup	85 grams
1 cup	340 grams

Oven Temperature

Fahrenheit	Celcius	Gas Mark
250 ºF	120 ºC	1/2
275 ºF	135 ºC	1
300 ºF	150 ºC	2
325 ºF	165 ºC	3
350 ºF	175 ºC	4
375 ºF	190 ºC	5
400 ºF	205 ºC	6
425 ºF	220 ºC	7
450 ºF	235 ºC	8
475 ºF	245 ºC	9
500 ºF	260 ºC	

The Story of Blue Osa

Marie is one of the original owners of the property where Blue Osa resides.

One day Yogi Aaron, who had been hosting a retreat in the area was driving with one of his students, Adam, who is now his business partner. Both were contemplating life beneath the vast Costa Rican sky and jungle canopy; daydreaming of setting up a dedicated retreat space. A place where people could relax. A place where people could savor stillness. And a place where people could safely question, "Who am I?"

Amid flourishing foliage and a dusty road haze sat a weather worn Century 21 sign. The pair intuitively pulled over -- life changed in that moment.

Despite being chased off the property by a feisty French lady and a trio of barking dogs, they didn't give up. They returned with a realtor who guided them through a majestic mess of jungle and sea and that's when they were officially introduced to Marie. Aaron and Adam fell in love with the potential of the property and knew it was the perfect place to create space for people to be themselves and offer life-changing, transformational yoga holidays.

Marie was inspired by Aaron and Adam's vision for a yoga sanctuary. The woman who once chased them away was now helping them set up the retreat. She quickly became an integral part of the family where she's fondly referred to as 'Mother' by everyone that comes to Blue Osa.

Born in Algeria and raised in the beach town of Biarritz in the south of France by a french mother and italian father, Marie is a self-taught chef, honing her culinary skills when her husband operated a French bistro in San Francisco and later an elegant French restaurant in Cartagena, Colombia.

To find out more about the story of Blue Osa visit: www.blueosa.com

BLUE OSA
yoga retreat + spa
playa tamales, osa peninsula, costa rica

A Labour of Love

This cookbook was an international labour of love. A dream turned into a reality by an international fusion of hearts and minds, blended together over the miles by their passion for good food and making things happen.

A team of seasoned writers, editors and photographers from around the world helped breathe life into Marie's book.

Who made it happen?

Chef Marie, who relentlessly compiled and tested a collection of her favourite recipes over many years.

Aaron and **Adam** at Blue Osa, who held the vision and trusted the process.

Randy Ferguson, who thumbed through thousands of recipes with Marie while singing French chanteuse songs and sipping tequila, all to bring her story to life. For pro pie tips, yoga retreat ideas, and creative marketing consulting, contact him at RandallJFerguson@gmail.com.

Katherine Smith, acting co-author, editor in chief and book producer, who journeyed from Europe to help turn the dream into a reality. Find out more; www.katherinesmithyoga.com

Maria Hillier, photographer extraordinaire who travelled all the way from Canada to capture the spirit of Blue Osa with her fabulous pictures. Find out more; http://mariahillierphotography.zenfolio.com

And the amazing graphic designer **Anine Cornelius Løvdal** from Norway pulled all the elements together to create the beautiful piece you're now holding in your hands. Find out more; send inquiries to aninec_lovdal@yahoo.com

Printed in the United States
by Baker & Taylor Publisher Services